MW01123294

God's Original Story of Love

Timeless Wisdom and Truth

God's Original Story of Love

written by
L. Bovolotto
M.Ed., M.A. Psych

Printed and distributed through Ingram Content Group.

First printing, 2021.

ISBN: 978-0-9937715-5-2 (Hardcover)
ISBN: 978-0-9937715-3-8 (Paperback)
ISBN: 978-0-9937715-4-5 (E-book)

The Story of Love as God originally intended.
Pure, simple and elegant.

It is with a reverent heart that I share these words of
wisdom with you. I offer this gift in the same spirit
as I received it from the Heart of the Universe,
with passion, grace and humility.

Contents

BOOK THREE   *An Invitation*

*Reverence
Raison d'Être*

Reverence – Raison d'Être

Once upon a heart …

Under the shade of a tree,
sat a dreamer

A dreamer of beauty and song
and all that is full with colour and form

In a moment of spontaneous stillness
all that this dreamer understood the world to be
vanished

And so, the dream began …

Images faded in and out as the dream unfolded
each image layered within another

A kaleidoscope of possibilities
offered on a platter of gold
to *honour* that which created all

No beginning, no end
no yesterday, no tomorrow
only the moment presented as a gift

Appreciated by the heart
felt as a joyful song
within, between, around

So goes, the dance of simply being
So goes, the dreamer and the dream

Moment by moment …

Cascading like the playful waterfall
Interwoven like the ever-reaching vine
Seeking like the sunflower to face the sun

Open – always open to …

The *offering*

Seeing, believing and knowing

Giving all in return; in a wave of honour and glory,
to that from which the offering came

The dance of love; the everlasting reciprocal wave of
receiving and giving

Joy and peace are forever yours!

BOOK ONE

Love

Love is a gift from the Heart of the Universe.

Love

I AM Love

I AM Love

Pure, simple and elegant. This is love. This is my heart – the Heart of the Universe which is given to you and to all, so that you may know your magnificence; so that you may know how to be with your brothers and sisters and all that crosses your path on your journey.

To love is to honour and treasure
your heart – our heart – the One Heart.

Keep it simple and let your heart guide you to a love so subtle, so pure and so magnificent that you weep tears of joy in its presence. Know that what you are witnessing is the majesty of love

love eternal

essence pure.

Be still and know that I AM love. I AM the one and only ode and vision of your heart. The song of your heart and the verse from your lips are all to glorify me – the Heart of the Universe – your one true love now and for all time.

I AM Love

Come to me chaste and pure of heart and know that all other pales in comparison to the love I hold for you. Like the bud of a flower, the love I hold for you will blossom from within your heart. Nurture and cherish this bud, the beginning of our loving relationship.

The love you have for yourself will provide the care and sustenance to bring your flower to full maturity.
To love so pure
    love as it was in the beginning
    love that creates, sustains and defines all.

Begin by watering the seeds of affection and tenderness towards yourself. With patience and care, only you can provide the conditions and space that allow your flower to sprout and blossom. Oh, the joy found with love in full bloom!

The love between you and your heart, there is no other love; the love that surrounds and embraces you comes from within your own heart.

I AM Love

The love you have for another, for beauty and peace and for the joy found in creative expression, comes from the love held in your heart for yourself. This love mirrors your relationship with the Heart of the Universe. This love resonates within us all.

Love yourself. That is all there is.
I AM love. Love is all.

In loving yourself you are bathed in and uplifted by
                    the magnificence of love
                    the I AM
                    the Heart of the Universe.
In loving yourself, you are loved in return. Your love of self, reflected back to you.

Since the beginning of time love has been and always will be the force behind
                    all creation and creativity
                    all reason and meaning
                    all desire and motivation
                    all beauty and circumstance
                    all life and decay.

See the world and universe through this new found perspective. Notice that nothing changes around you except your understanding of who you are in relation to others and the world.

All is love. All created from love. When you see the world through the eyes of your heart, you will recognize this truth. Although, you can manipulate, shape and reconfigure everything into different forms, trust that it is all part of the original seed. Everything originated from love – the seed of my heart.

It is your perspective that transforms or appears to transform others, places, things. When you see through the eyes of love
the eyes of your heart – all becomes clear
                        all appears as love.

Pure, simple, and elegant.

This is the beginning of a new relationship between you and your heart and the world around you. In this moment, clarity begins to emerge and you are given a glimpse of the vision – the intention that was for all in the beginning; the desire of the Heart of the Universe for all creation.

All … created from love
       sustained by love
       simply is as love.

As it was in the beginning, is now and will be forevermore.

Love

Part II

Part II

The seed of love that was in the beginning was given to all so that they may know how to simply be present, aware and surrounded by my love.

This seed of love is potent and pure. It began as
> a twinkle in the night sky
> a spark of my imagination
> a creative instinct.

Like the bird, that knows how to build its nest in preparation for its young. It lays each twig in a resourceful fashion to build a nest that is unique; with instinct, creativity and timing of the seasons.

A twinkle, a spark – the inception of all began with the seed of my imagination as it opened to reveal the flower of life.

And so it was, from the darkness the spark alit; the basis for all life and form ignited by the power and passion of love, to burn brightly forevermore. Every star that graces the universe was born of this spark, each dancing to glorify my presence.

The dance of love; twinkling
                    sparkling; the passionate burning of
the flame that lights the universe. Where there once was
darkness, now light.

The torch passed from star to new star, lighting up
    the heavens
    the universal expanse
with the light and love of the Heart of the Universe.
Glorious and majestic; burning brightly in honour of
that which created the spark and the moment that dark
became light.

The stars created in the beginning continue to grace the
universe. Their presence is an everlasting reminder of
                    the spark
                    the light
                    the love that lives within all.

Each star given its moment of glory at the time of its
birth as a new star; its birth fueled by the passion of the
star that preceded it. Each star, unique and called by
name.

Each star a descendant of the original spark; the original intention of the Heart of the Universe to share the love held by the One Heart.

In a dance of praise the stars formed patterns that were pleasing, each formation a tribute to the One Heart; twinkling, dancing and burning brightly in adoration to the source of all creation.

In witnessing this, the Heart of the Universe was pleased. And so, it happened that from love came love. Love emanated from the One Heart and returned in kind; full circle in a wave of light.

Pure, simple and elegant.

Love as light; radiant beams streaming across the universe. Each ray a beautiful expression of the love of the Heart of the Universe.

And so, it remained for a time. The stars expanded, multiplied, and filled the universe with light, beauty and the love so generously shared by the Heart of the Universe.

Love

Part III

Part III

The stars continued to shine brightly against the dark backdrop of the nothingness that was before their creation. In a moment of joy, the stars began to sing. In a wave that spanned the universe, they joined in harmony, resonating with the love that created them.

In honour of the One Heart, the stars sent flares of light and fine luminous dust across the great expanse. In a wave of knowing, the dust gathered and shaped once again by the creative imagination of the Heart of the Universe.

Within each grain of sand lay a seed − the flower of life waiting to emerge. Like the paint that graces the canvas with each brushstroke, the seeds of life awaken to grace the universe with the breath of life; the breath of the Heart of the Universe.

With each moment
        each breath, the Heart of the Universe delights in creating on a new canvas, with a rainbow of colours from which to choose.

Part III

With each breath a wave of love
                a seed planted
                a new life
                a new form
                a new presence.

Pleased with its creation the One Heart inhaled and in the moment of exhalation invited the grain of sand, that contained the seed of life, to take the form of moons, planets and comets to blaze a trail in a demonstration of the fiery passion of love within the One Heart.

And so, where there once was darkness, life began to take form; each star, planet and moon blessed with the seeds of life; each a celebration of the One Heart from which they were created.

Like the flower that blooms in its own time, each seed would sprout when the conditions were right; the birth of each seed as part of the melodic dance of the universe with a unique voice in the universal symphony; each knowing the timing of this well choreographed score.

Part III

Each step in perfect resonance with the Heart of the Universe; no thought required – only attunement to the rhythm of the One Heart; inborn, instinctual and ever-present in the heart of every seed.

Much like a compass set to due north, each heart is set to recognize and attune to the Heart of the Universe; pure, simple and elegant.

The planets, moons and stars found their place and rejoiced in the masterpiece before them. Beautifully choreographed, each knew their part in the dance – in the universal symphony; no question or doubt, only absolute certainty in the miracle and mystery of creation.

All corners of the universe filled with love, beauty, song and graceful movement. All were grateful for simply being present as part of the creative, playful imagination of the Heart of the Universe – as love displayed in physical form. And so, it remained for a time.

Love

Part IV

Part IV

With each inhalation and exhalation, the universe came alive. The cycle of birth, decay and rebirth began. This initiated other cycles in turn. The planets began to spin, the movement of the stars took on a cyclical dance and the luminous dust from the star flares found its place in the cycle of life.

So it began, graceful
        grace-filled movement
all orchestrated by the creative imagination of the Heart of the Universe. It began with the simplest of cycles − the inhalation and exhalation of the One Heart. With each breath, the universe took on different shapes and forms; all part of the playful and joy-filled dance of creative imagination.

The seeds of life began to sprout each in their own time; each life given their moment of glory. Like the evening primrose that bursts open in a ceremonial display of colour and form, from dusk to dawn, away from the spotlight; a quiet celebration between each seed and the Heart of the Universe.

Each life form emerged from the darkness.
From the seed
  the womb
  the earth
  the depth of the universe; a mystery tucked away
ready to reveal its beauty
    its magnificence. All rejoiced along with the Heart of the Universe, the moment the mystery unveiled itself; a moment of joy in witnessing the miracle of life – the miracle of creation.

Peace filled and covered the earth, chosen by the One Heart to sprout the seeds of life. Each new creation and new life form recognized, cherished and blessed by the Heart of the Universe.

Each seed and form called by name and invited
  to glorify that which created it
  to honour itself
  to honour all created from love.
Each seed
  in perfect harmony and pitch
  in perfect resonance with the One Heart.

Part IV

Land, water and succulents emerged all in perfect harmony and balance. The land took form in varied shapes, sizes, textures and colours
>> to delight the senses of those to follow
>> to support and provide the necessities of life.
The water
> nectar of life, flowed throughout the earth filling in the open areas and every space and crevice of the land.

The land and water became acquainted, joining in a song of praise and gratitude to the One Heart for they knew their purpose. They understood their place in the universal masterpiece; to support and nurture life to come. Joyfully and joy-filled the land and water graciously accepted and stood before the One Heart with love for that which created them.

The water and land entertained themselves for a time while the succulents took root, finding places for new life to begin. This time was playful and creative while the Heart of the Universe paused for the next breath – the next inhalation and exhalation.

Love

Part V

Part V

And, so it was that the earth continued to take form. Everything was a reflection of the love of the One Heart; a reminder of the love that created all from a spark of creative imagination. Pure, simple and elegant.

The seeds of life took hold in the darkness; in the womb of the earth. Each seed sprouted in its own moment of glory, maturing with the cycles of the moon and stars. Life reached out to meet the light, and in the darkness rested. So, it was in this way, that the earth began to bloom.

Each sprout became a living testament to the Heart of the Universe; each containing the original seed

> the flower of life
> the spark of love.

Like the stars that passed the torch

> the light of love, life begat
life; passing on the seeds of the blessed flower of life to continue forevermore. All corners of the earth sprouted with the vividness, passion and luminosity of the stars that came before them.

Part V

The spark of life in varied size, shape, texture and colour to delight the senses, a gift of love from the One Heart.

The cycle of birth, decay and rebirth followed the natural rhythm and pulse of the universe, attuned to the heartbeat of the Heart of the Universe. The stars, planets, moons and new life aligned themselves to this pulse; the heartbeat that signaled the way

to the truth
to the light
to love.

With each breath, the Heart of the Universe scattered the seeds across the earth. The land, ripe and ready, received the seeds and welcomed them into its folds. There they remained until coaxed by the light to emerge and turn their face to the light – the One Heart.

Each seed, bud and flower attuned to the light, simply knowing that the light was the way to the Heart of the Universe. Pure, simple and elegant. The masterpiece continued to unfold.

Part V

In the next moment, the breath of the Heart of the Universe flowed on this wave of knowing and gave all life the gift of its breath.

With each inhalation and exhalation of the One Heart, all life would now respond in kind; the breath of the Heart of the Universe regulating and guiding the breath of all life. Each breath riding the wave of light – the ecstasy of love – was now an intricate part of the creation of the Heart of the Universe.

Like a playful dance, a wave of knowing swept across the earth and the universe. There was a quiet reverence and gratitude for the One Heart. In response, the Heart of the Universe sent a wave of love that blanketed all; a reciprocal wave of gratitude, reverence and love.

Magnificent – a masterpiece!

And so, it remained for a time, the earth adorned with the beauty of life. The first breaths of life – the breath of the Heart of the Universe – given to all life so they may flow on the wave of light
the wave of love.

Love

Part VI

Part VI

To complete the cycle of birth, decay and rebirth, the Heart of the Universe added another element to the earth. The breath of life shared with the creatures that would roam the earth. They too, would be born of the seed of love, from the spark of creative imagination of the Heart of the Universe.

Like the spark ignited by the power and passion of love, each creature would be born of the passion and love of the creature that preceded it. All born of the love held within the One Heart; each birth given its moment of glory as part of creation.

Like the seeds that sprouted from the land, the seeds that would bear the creatures were scattered across all corners of the earth. The creatures would roam the earth, move in the waters and soar amid the breath of life.

The earth and all that surrounded the earth would be blessed with the seeds of life; with the love of the Heart of the Universe to sing, dance and play as part of creation, now and forevermore.

All would live in harmony. The stars, moons, planets, land, water and life that inhabited the earth, all filled with the love contained in the original spark; all in balance with the breath – the flow of the inhalation and exhalation of the Heart of the Universe.

With each inhalation, the light would shine and with each exhalation, the dark would pervade; each breath signaling a time for play and a time for rest.

With each inhalation all life
> invited to turn their face toward the light
> toward the One Heart
> in gratitude for the love shared with all.

Each exhalation allowed for
> a pause
>
> a moment of quiet preparation for the new to be born in the darkness; born of the creative imagination of the One Heart
>
> a seed to be planted in the womb of the earth and the womb of each creature on the earth.

Part VI

The cycles were set.

Abundance flowed across the earth and throughout the universe. The gifts of life

  of light

  of love were given by the Heart of the Universe, to be shared by all. Love flowed within, between and around all, enveloping and immersing all creation in love, peace and joy.

The Heart of the Universe pleased with its creation paused and rested. The seeds sprouted from the earth and the creatures multiplied. The dance of life began, as participants knew their place; all beautifully choreographed by the One Heart.

And so, it remained for a long while. The Heart of the Universe delighted. The creatures of the earth were humbled and grateful for this paradise created
by a spark of imagination
by love itself.

Love

Part VII

Part VII

A pause …
A moment of rest
      of quiet reflection.
A tribute to oneself
      to the eternal heart
      to the Heart of the Universe.

Pleased with its creation, the Heart of the Universe paused to reflect and honour the stars, planets, moons and life that now inhabited the earth and the universe. The magnificence of the One Heart reflected back upon itself.

Love witnessing love!

Playful, joyful and receptive; all throughout the universe open to receiving the love offered by the Heart of the Universe.

Loving, tender and gracious; the Heart of the Universe generously bestowed its love upon all. Oh, to witness this magnificent reciprocal relationship; the dance of love!

Part VII

In this cycle of rest, the Heart of the Universe invited all to join in the celebration of the new creation; the creation of life and love eternal. All were asked to rejoice in the miracle of creative imagination — imagination centered on love; all created from, by and with love.

Everything a reflection of the Heart of the Universe
a reflection of love.
Each moment spent in quiet celebration of the One Heart was a moment to rejoice in life itself.

During this period of contemplation and celebration, the Heart of the Universe took the seed of life and graced it with the gift of imagination.

Filled with the love of the Heart of the Universe, the life that emerged from these seeds

would *understand and honour*
the gift of creative imagination
would *honour and cherish* all life that
was created by the Heart of the Universe.

Part VII

Blessed with the gift of imagination these seeds

> would *act* as the One Heart on earth
>
> would *be responsible* for the continued creation according to the initial intention
>
> would *honour* the intention as originally envisioned by the Heart of the Universe.

Each breath, step and vision of the seeds created from the original seed of love, would be aligned with that of the Heart of the Universe.

Each seed called by name and given

> a unique place on the earth
>
> a special purpose to fulfill and sustain the vision held by the One Heart.

The earth, as part of the universe, would radiate love, peace and joy. The land, water, sprouts, creatures and the new seeds endowed with the gift of imagination would all align harmoniously with the Heart of the Universe.

Part VII

Creation graced with the power to create. The new seeds given influence over that which was shared by all. In using this influence, power and gift of imagination, the Heart of the Universe requested that all be done

   in the name of the One Heart that created all

   in the name of love.

So it was, that the seeds would multiply and share the gift of imagination with their offspring; each subsequent birth

   a *testament* to the One Heart

   a *vow* to continue to create paradise on earth.

Beauty, abundance, joy, peace and love offered to all by the Heart of the Universe, and reoffered by the seeds of love that bore themselves.

Hallelujah!
Love begat love!
Love is all!

BOOK TWO

In the Beginning

Let this gift from the Heart of the Universe
be your guide to the truth, the light and the way.

In the Beginning - Part I

The Vision

The Vision

Through this blessed hand, I have a voice.

Let me share with you my vision for all existence. It is this vision that allowed all to take form. Each plant, animal, flare, ray — all that is — came from my imagination. I am part of everything that is visible and invisible.

This is how I intimately know all.
I am all. I created all. I AM the Creator.

> *In the beginning, all was one with the source of all creation. There was no fear or uncertainty.*
>
> *In the beginning, your heart and the Heart of the Universe beat in unison at the rhythmic vibration of love; love that is boundless, fearless, joyful and forever faithful.*
>
> *In the beginning, your heart recognized the innate beauty and goodness in all. You understood the gift of life and the joy found in the fullness of creative expression.*

This creative expression as one with me creates beauty, joy, balance and love among all that exists. As you sing, dance and play as one, the universe is in perfect pitch and balance.

When you turn your face – your heart towards me, you will see the vision held in my heart for all.

When you give yourself completely to this vision held in the beginning, you will see who I AM in you.

When you allow all held in your honour to be absorbed into your being, you will know who I AM.

I live in you and you live in me. Together, in a unified vision, each of you will bring forth my luminous presence. Breathe me in; with each inhalation and exhalation, feel my presence within and around your being.

This is truth entering and surrounding you.
This is love.

In the Beginning - Part II

The Part Within

The Part Within

There is a part within
      that seeks
      that sees
      that believes
      that knows

Awaken this part within
      that seeks
      that sees
      that believes
      that knows

Befriend this part within
      that seeks
      that sees
      that believes
      that knows

Become this part within
      that seeks
      that sees
      that believes
      that knows

The Part Within

Seek

Seek

Simple, uncomplicated and unfettered. Let your heart guide you to what your mind seeks.

The mind gifted to all that breathe and walk on this earth; given so that those who have the ability to sense may delight in the beauty before them.

The mind in its simplicity attempts to seek what can only be found through the heart. Like the blind mole, the mind roots around seeking to find that which is not visible. Without the vision of the heart the mind will forever be shielded from the truth.

The mind will dig itself
        deeper and deeper into confusion.
        Data, figures
        experiences, opinions
        gestures and platitudes
all because the mind seeks.

Like the snake that swallows its own tail, the mind will discover that even if all were digested and re-digested over and over, the answers would remain the same.

Seek

The mystery of the universe is unsolvable. Mystery is what entertains and livens up your existence.

It is all a mystery.

> *It is all a mystery* — how life began; how a flower blooms in every variety of colour, scent and style.

> *The mystery will continue to unravel for all eternity.* As soon as a satisfactory answer appears, another mystery follows.

> *The focus of the mystery* is not the unraveling, rather the power of and reverence for the magnificence of life.

The mystery asks that you pause and reflect on the undeniable truth that lies at the Heart of the Universe.

It is this truth that the mind seeks, but only
                    the heart can reveal.
Let your mind stand in awe as it witnesses the beauty and joy found by allowing your heart to lead you home.

The Part Within

Awaken

Awaken

You are the seeker
> the knower
> the truth.

Within you lie all the secrets of the universe. Like the stars that twinkle with ancient wisdom of civilizations past, know that you carry this wisdom within.

It is through me that you will awaken to this truth. I have given you your heart. It is attuned to my heart. It beats in unison to the natural rhythm of the universe.

Your heart knows the way.

All that you have envisioned and shaped on the earth is but a fragment of what is possible.

Take my hand and let me guide you.

Let me show you the vision held in the beginning for all. Simple, just, and majestic; bathed in love and joy. A vision fit for the kings and queens that inhabit this kingdom. Come home to this sacred vision that I held and continue to hold for each of you and for all on earth and throughout the universe.

Open the eyes of your heart and join me. Together as one we will recreate paradise.

You look to each other to find the answer. Only through me, who created all you see, will find the answers you seek. Awaken to this truth.

The images you have created of beings supreme distract you from the beauty and truth that lives within you. I made each of you in my own image. You are magnificent! All I ask of you is to remember and wake up to this truth.

It is only through me that you come to understand your place in the universal dance of love
> the dance of your heart
> the dance of joy
> the dance of simple perfection
> the dance of righteousness
> the dance that connects all
in a wave of knowing.

By taking part in the universal dance, you may join others on earth and throughout the universe in a celebration, in honour of your heart and new beginnings. Stand with your heart-eyes open, ready to receive the blessings, joy and love that awaits you.

The love I hold for each of you
                    my children

                    my sweet innocent babes is immeasurable, pure and everlasting. Let me show you the way back to the *hallelujah*, your rightful place among the kings and queens that came before you. Awaken!

The Part Within

See

See

Grace that comes from the all-knowing and all-seeing is given to you so that you may see through my eyes all that is.

Let the eyes of your heart open to what is real. Your physical eyes see only the reflection, a subtle glimpse, of your true beauty. See the rose in full bloom as a celebration of the beauty within you.

Be present and aware of all that comes before you. Like a storybook unfolding, the details of your journey will reveal themselves to you.

The eyes of your heart are wise and discerning. They know and understand truth. They sift and organize all information in an instant with the precision of a hawk's eye with quick

      decisive action

      instinctual with no thought.

Observe these creatures, as they will show you this natural way of being; clear and focused with their eyes transfixed on the treasure. In that moment all else fades away.

See

Your heart knows without thought or analysis what, where and how it must respond.

Keep your heart-eyes focused, clear and directed only at me; nothing else matters. The wisdom of the truth and what you seek can only be found through the eyes of your heart.

Your heart – our heart
Your eyes – my eyes

They are one and the same.

Focus all your attention and see this truth in everything you observe, from the grain of sand to the mighty oak tree. It does not matter what you choose to focus on as I AM in all.

All you need to do is pause long enough to see this truth. It is right before you and always has been. Stop, breathe, look and see with the eyes of your heart and voilà there I AM.

See

Simple, beautiful and elegant; see clearly the miracle of all life on earth and throughout the universe. I have made it delightfully easy.

The animals that walk the earth do not question or doubt. Do not let the power I have bestowed upon you become that which keeps you from me. It was given to you so that you could share my truth

my light, with all.

This power is a gift. See through my eyes how to use it wisely. The eyes of your heart will guide you to this vision I have for all humanity. Thank you for taking a moment to pause and see the truth of who I AM in you.

The Part Within

Befriend

Befriend

Quivering with anticipation, the desire of your heart is to know me. First, we must become reacquainted. Stand quietly before me and glance at your reflection.

At first glance the brilliance
            the radiance, will ignite the spark of love that lives within your heart. Your heart will recognize this as truth
      as love.

With time this vision of your magnificence will soften and deepen. You will come to know and befriend all that you are. The initial discomfort of meeting your one true love again — for what feels like the first time — will pass with each encounter.

The hesitation you feel is in part your heart's understanding and respect held for the reverence and sacredness of life. Your heart is a gateway to all the secrets of the universe. The key to that opening lies in your willingness to offer your attention and commitment to the awareness of who you are in the sacred dance of birth, death and rebirth.

Befriend

Joyful, loving and graceful is the dance of love between you and your heart. Allow this dance of acceptance and ease to fill your being. Speak softly
                    sing sweetly
                    caress gently your inner beauty
and tenderly extend an invitation to come out and play.

Breathe me in.
Breathe out love.
Simply joyous.

With our re-acquaintance in its infancy, it is most important to find quiet moments to hear the calling of your heart. Each breath signals an opportunity for a chance meeting.

A glimpse at first; a moment to linger; stay awhile and feel the loving embrace of your dearest friend
                    your confidant
                    your all.
Only you alone can initiate this meeting and only you alone can sustain the relationship that binds our hearts together.

Befriend

Listen as you are invited to open the eyes of your heart
and see the face of a friend
> the flower in bloom
> an animal approaching
> the home filled with joy
> the world lightened with laughter
> the universe rejoicing in song.

It begins with a quiver

a moment of ecstasy between you and
your heart. This gift of friendship is my gift to you.
Treasure this offering as a mother who holds her
newborn child across her breast. Hold it dear and know
that it is what brings you to me and connects us for all
eternity.

The Part Within

Believe

Believe

Together as one, we share the same vision; the vision I hold for all on earth and throughout the universe. Your belief in this truth will guide you to know who I AM in you. This belief will shatter all preconceived notions of separation and the need for individual will.

The dance of our heart is light and joyous. Our song whispers sonatas across the universe. Our touch sends ripples of ecstasy to all that cross our path. The very thing I desire for you is what your heart desires.

Believe, believe, believe.

All that is, is right before you. The glimpses I have shared will ignite the spark of truth and knowing from within. Your belief will fan the embers to release the passion and hunger to be as one with me.

This belief lies beneath all the bravado and fanfare. Quietly coax and welcome your magnificence to reveal itself. As your belief in who you are strengthens, your spark will burn brightly and your commitment to our vision will be honoured.

Believe

Stroke your flame gently with the care and attention given to a rare orchid. Your consistent and unwavering belief will provide the fuel needed to keep the flame aglow.

How beautiful this fire that burns! Let it shine for all to see. May it ignite the spark of truth and surety from within that what lives in you, lives in them, lives in all.

Belief is like fruit on a forbidden tree. Once it is tasted it no longer remains belief but a constant insecurity and questioning of what could have been. Left alone, with a trusting heart, the fruit becomes a symbol of your faith and belief in me.

Remain in your heart with your eyes towards me and do not be tempted by the taste of power and desire to know. This will be given to you as the fruit ripens and your flame matures. With patience, care and the belief that you deserve love immeasurable, all will be given to you.

Trust and honour yourself and believe that each bud, each blossom, each tree has its own reason for being.

This understanding will become clearer with each step you take towards seeing and knowing this truth for yourself.

This is yours alone to do
    naked and free of all fear or uncertainty
    surrounded by the flame of burning desire to be one with me. The path to my heart is only a breath away. Receive this truth with each breath you take. Have faith and let our flame burn brightly. Believe!

The Part Within

Become

Become

This next step in your heart's journey anchors your commitment to your heart

        our heart

        the Heart of the Universe. To become this part that you seek from within, you must understand and acknowledge the sacredness of all life and existence.

I will show you the way to the hallelujah

           the moment of rejoicing throughout the universe as you take your rightful place amongst the stars, planets, moons and suns that grace the universe. They are the kings and queens of civilizations past. You, too, will join in glorifying the Heart of the Universe with your stately presence.

Rejoice in knowing that you have a place that is uniquely yours. It has and always will be here waiting for the moment you choose to honour and cherish your heart.

All will sing in praise of this glorious moment as you remember your magnificence! This moment of remem-

Become

brance coincides with the instant you become reunited with the Heart of the Universe
        Heart to heart.
As you stand transfixed, you know in this moment that your heart and the Heart of the Universe are one and the same. You have become the truth that your heart longs to find.

In answering yes to the call of your heart – to the call of the Heart of the Universe, you allow your heart to guide you home. Remain focused, aware and committed to the desire of your heart.

Bless the journey of your heart with a thankful appreciation. Each twist and turn further reveals your truth, making it possible to trust and commit to your heart. All will be revealed in its own time.

Day after day
month after month
year after year, watch with amazement as the synchronistic moments reveal your life's purpose. What you are being asked to become will grow to be clear.

Become

The seduction of the heart and the ecstasy of knowing, stir the longing inside to seek and discover the mystery of the universe. Know who you are and allow yourself to fully become, honour and accept your responsibility in the universal masterpiece; exquisite

> extraordinary
> magnificent
> a reflection of you.

Peace and joy forevermore await you when you decide to join the others before you in the universal heart song that celebrates who you are. It is in this moment that you become the part within

> the hallelujah.

The Part Within

Know

Know

The hallelujah! Tears of joy! The deep knowing from within that what you are experiencing is truth. This and so much more awaits you.

With each *yes*

each confirmation that your heart makes to honour, cherish and bless your truth, you move closer to seeing and experiencing all of who you are. You simply know that this is truth before you

this is you.

Stand still and quietly acknowledge your magnificence. In honouring yourself, you honour all throughout the universe for you are truth

you are beauty
you are joy
you are peace and understanding
you are all.

When you know this with all your being, you understand your responsibility to love, honour and cherish yourself.

Know

Be truth
speak truth
live truth. This becomes a natural way of being when
you know that you are truth.

Rejoice and celebrate the moment your heart accepts
and acknowledges that this is so. This is the moment
that

the Heart of the Universe welcomes you home;

you know your place in the universal dance;

*you release your heart song and allow it to guide your
steps and the flow of your movement.*

Sing, dance and play in the truth, knowing that you are
a blessed child of the Heart of the Universe. All has all
been created for you to enjoy. The Heart of the
Universe delights in witnessing your joy.

Use the gift of your senses to take in all the beauty and
sensual pleasures that surround you. This is all yours
for simply knowing and honouring all of who you are.

Know

Eagerly accept all that is given, with a heart filled with *gratitude and reverence* for all that has been created and generously offered to you and to all.

Walk lightly and simply in this truth
the truth.

Know that you are loved beyond what your mind and body can comprehend. It is only through your heart that you know, without question, the purity and depth of the love that is held sacred and dear for you and for all throughout the universe.

I, the Creator of all
the Heart of the Universe, ask that you also hold this knowing dear to your heart. Know that I AM and always will be the truth
the light
the way.

Hallelujah!

The Part Within

I AM – So It Is

I AM – So It Is

Seek no more. I AM – so it is.

I AM the answer to all questions
to all creation
to all you seek to know.

Although you stand before me and witness your reflection, your magnificence, it will take time for your mind and body to accept the magnitude of the glory you are witnessing. Be patient, gentle and kind with yourself as you digest the reality
the truth present before you.

Smile and rejoice. Keep it simple and pure. The answers you seek are not yours to uncover. They will remain the mystery of the Heart of the Universe.

Like a child who knows the limits of their responsibility, yours is to cherish the gifts given to you; the gifts of sensing, knowing and feeling as you become and simply be as one with that which created you.

I AM – So It Is

Spend your days
     your nights
     your life, with your face
          with your heart turned toward the
I AM, in praise for all that is given on earth and
throughout the universe.

It has been given so that you may remember and see
the I AM in all that surrounds you. Let every tree, river,
flower, song and sunrise remind you of who I AM in
you.

I have made it delightfully easy for all to know who
I AM for I live in each of you
        I live in all
        I AM all.

Your life was created to worship me
              the I AM within you.
In loving and honouring yourself, your heart extends
words of praise to the One Heart
        the Heart of the Universe
        the I AM.

I AM – So It Is

Put aside the part within you that longs to find me in the sun, moon and river strong. These are but glimpses of who I AM in you. Come stand before me completely bare and I will show you how to be present in mind, body and heart as one with me

the Heart of the Universe.

Together we will light up the world, the universe and beyond that which exists in the present moment. Let me bathe you in the hallelujah now and forevermore.

This is love.
This is joy.
This is peace.

I AM – so it is!
Sing, dance and play as you rejoice in this truth. Amen!

BOOK THREE

An Invitation

To those that long to answer *yes*
to the call of their heart.
A loving conversation awaits …

An Invitation - Part I

Truth

Truth

Innocence

Child of Mine

I extend for you
an opportunity to
bathe yourself in my light
life will become joyous

See beyond
the layers upon layers
of heaviness that has
obscured your knowing of me

With each moment
of letting go
my image evolves with clarity
and you become less doubtful

Light within radiates outward
with purity and innocence
as you awaken the beauty inside
and lovingly share it with others

Embrace the opportunities
to intimately discover
who I AM within you
my beloved

Innocence

Let me introduce myself
    I AM
    I am the breath of life
    I am the living light
    I am the spark of divine love within you. I came into this world as a receptive, loving, curious, responsive and changing essence. I am vibrant and fully present in the moment. I move with grace and form a unique relationship with all I meet. My desire is to shine for all to see.

I am the innocence that remains hidden beneath the adult constructs you may have felt were necessary to survive in this world. I occasionally peak out as a child too bashful to be seen. The invitation is always there, for you to acknowledge your child-like loving innocence.

I patiently anticipate the moment when you breathe life into every experience and allow all of who I am to be birthed through you. Like the newborn with its first cry of presence in this world, you are blessed with the ability to express yourself openly and freely through me.

Innocence

It is through you I come alive.

See through my eyes, the beauty in each person you meet. Our gentle gaze will be a mirror for what you recognize in others.

Feel my gentle caress as it melts your heart and brings tears of joy. Together the touch of our hand will extend a graceful note of compassion and peace to other hearts.

Listen and hear my voice as that of a friend and lover. The sound of our voice will be like music that others are drawn towards.

The clarity of my words will help you come to an inner wisdom and unquestionable knowing. Our words will be spoken from a place of simplicity that is recognized by others as truth.

Come and breathe my familiar sweet fragrance. The light aromatic quality of our presence is welcoming to others.

Join me

the spark of divine love

the living light

the breath of life within you and the Creator of all, as you discover who you are. Take my hand and let me guide you. I will walk lightly by your side as a constant friend who intimately knows the light and the wisdom of truth that lives within you.

Open your mind and heart and let us begin our journey together. Trust that I am always present to lead the way. Through me your strength will shine and be seen as *grace, wisdom and compassion.*

Come walk with me …

Truth

Awaken

.

First Step

Let the intense
desire from within
guide you to
your heart's awakening

The heart seeks
to reveal itself
as an intimate
friend and lover

Take the first step
by creating quiet
open space
to listen with reverence

In the solitude
away from the spotlight
the heart unwraps
itself before you

Unbounded joy
is unleashed as
the heart is recognized
and cherished

Awaken

It is time to wake up from your slumber as there is much to experience in this life.

The choice is yours.

You can continue sleeping or respond to the opportunity offered to you. This is a gift to you from the Heart of the Universe so that you may awaken to who you truly are.

Listen as your heart invites you

to *bless and cherish* the body which contains your essence

to *welcome* the face before you as a friend

to *nurture* the earth, supporting the delicate balance of life

to *cleanse* the air with every breath you take

to *bathe* all with light as purified by your thoughts, words and actions.

Everything that comes before you is an opportunity to observe and recognize where this lives in you. Curiously explore with the excitement, wonderment and innocence you experienced as a child.

I am always present and willing to assist you in the process of awakening. Allow your heart to open and reveal your inner wisdom. Let the infinite wisdom of who you are expand your awareness.

Picture the most precious treasure you have in your life at this moment. Take it or an image of its likeness into your hand and place it on your heart. This treasure you are acknowledging is reflective of your beauty within – your essence. There are many choices. Choose what you wish to reflect.

As you awaken choose to surround yourself with the people, objects and experiences that make your heart sing. This is your song
          our song
          the universal song
that glorifies all of who you are.

The universe awaits and rejoices as you recognize and welcome the unique melody of your song. Listen as the wisdom of your heart asks you to follow your song. It resonates within and invites you to create harmony with the songs of others and all that exists.

The invitation to participate in this magnificent vibrational harmony is offered to you and to all on earth and throughout the universe.

Seize the opportunity gifted to you in each moment. Say *yes* with each breath you take. Awaken so you may become aware of who you truly are. The *choice is yours.*

Truth

Inner Beauty

Trust Me

Follow me my child

As I lead you
to your inner majesty
Your heart weeps at the
sight of the beauty before you

It is difficult to
comprehend that you
Are the embodiment
of the light being witnessed

Trust me my child

This is the truth
This is the divine
This is you

Inner Beauty

Magnificence! Oh, to show you what I see in you.

You are a masterpiece
        an exquisite beauty. This is echoed back in all
that you sense. Your senses open you to the presence
of beauty within you and in everything around you.
Take notice as you step into each picturesque gallery on
earth.

Remember that everything you are witnessing is a
reflection of what lives in you. These things have been
presented to you in ways so that they can enter in
through the knowing of your heart.

Let these wondrous manifestations awaken you to
recognize your beauty. Sit quietly amongst them and
watch. I will lay my hand on your heart and show you
your magnificence.

Through me, you may come to know
your inner beauty
your truth
your unique melody in the universal symphony.

Inner Beauty

Like the cascading waterfall, your essence is subtle yet so immense. It easily slips from your grasp, yet has the power to soften even the hardest of matter.

Your song like the air can be but a slight breeze or a gale that can release all barriers in its path. Recognize that through me you can express your tender, gentle nature but also your strength to conquer all that keeps you from me.

Find that delicate balance within you, just as the exotic flower presents itself as an exquisite beauty despite the tropical storms that threaten its existence. Your strength lies in knowing the truth of who you are and in the commitment you make to honour this truth, the same truth that is your divine power.

It is this power that supports you and allows you the freedom to express your subtle, delicate essence; the very essence that shines its light so it may be reflected back.

Inner Beauty

Begin to see through my eyes and witness the radiant light that lives within you. Let this light be an ever-present reminder of your inner beauty

your brilliance.

Let it shine for all to see so they may also be reminded of who they are.

It is only in the *recognition of your magnificence* that you are able to reflect this and witness it in others. When you come to know and experience your magnificence, together we can radiate the light

the truth

the beauty of who you are

who I am in you.

Truth

Seeking Truth

Pure Intention

Pure heart
seeker of truth
Feel the universal
knowing within

Lightened heart
keeper of wisdom
Gratefully shared
with all

Illumined heart
one with light
See blessings
joy, paradise

Universal Heart
eternally beats in
Unified rhythm of
pure consciousness

Seeking Truth

Here I AM – stand still. Wherever you go, I am there with you. I have been with you since the beginning of time. I am the truth, the light and the way. As you awaken from your sleep you will come to know I am truth in you.

Allow your heart to become a pure, open vessel of light that recognizes this truth within. Your truth is my truth and is the same truth that lives in everything here on earth and throughout the universe. You need not look far to find it, as truth is within and all around you. You are truth.

Like the birds who know to awaken at sunrise, you too know how to awaken to the truth. In your dreams both conscious and unconscious, I have given you reminders of who you are.

Let your innocent heart open to all that is around you. Everything you sense and engage is a signpost encouraging you to awaken to the truth. All your heart asks is that you notice and acknowledge these reminders that point the way to the truth in you.

Seeking Truth

Watch the children as they will direct you to this knowing. See it in their eyes, hear it in their voice and feel it in their warm embrace. As a child in the place of open connection to the truth, connect with all living things from the heart in the present moment.

As you begin to live in your truth – the truth – you may notice lightness and playfulness in your relationships and all you do. Life becomes filled with mystery and fascination as you look for clues and messages in this earthly playground.

Seek not to compete with others in this mysterious adventure, as all are celebrated that choose to take part in the play of physical form here on earth. Trust that each heart has a unique place in this playful, joyful dance rooted in truth.

See this life as enchanting with abundant opportunities for you to envision your reality. You have the power to manifest a joyous life with an inexplicable inner peace.

With each breath *choose* to seek only truth. Know that what your heart seeks and desires is the same truth that exists in all. This has been, is now and will forever be your heart's desire. The very thing your heart desires is the very thing I wish for you.

It is only in the recognition of your truth, that others may join you in a joyful dance and create paradise here on earth. This is possible by coming together with a clear vision and knowing of truth within. Find delight in the endless possibilities as you seek the truth, the light and the way.

All this awaits you and is available in the place where you presently stand. Stand still – here I AM.

An Invitation - Part II

Truths of Mind,
Body, Spirit

Truths of Mind, Body, Spirit

The truths of mind, body and spirit are infinite just as the universe is infinite. Let the truths presented here be signposts on your journey in the discovery of who you are. Allow them to be a guiding light on your path. Look to the wisdom of the stars and the endless colours of the rainbow to paint your world. Know that I am there with every step you take.

You are the light, the truth

Love is your divine power

Trust your intuition

Commitment to truth

Surrender your will to divine will

We are not separate

Live in the present moment

Let go of all

Breathe

You are the light, the truth

Rainbow Child

I am the light
that dwells within
a rainbow of colours
to brush your world

Imagine
red – orange – yellow
green – blue – violet
hues from which to choose

Endless possibilities

Passionately create
your unique self
to shine for all to see

Love is your divine power

GOD

God's power is love
God is love

In your human-ness
love is indescribable
and unfathomable

To be in the presence of love
even if only momentarily
is life altering

Love has the power to
soften the heart
bringing you onto bended
knee

To aspire to love another
is all you can
ask of yourself

Trust your intuition

Let Me Guide

Let me be your eyes
when life becomes
a blurry haze

Let me be your ears
when the noisy confusion
muffles my voice

Let me be your voice
when you hesitate
in speaking your truth

Let me nourish your heart
when it cries out
for sustenance and support

Trust me my child

Rest in my arms
and let me be your guide

Commitment to truth

All of You

*As you wander
down paths
presented as choices*

*Let your heart guide you
as a beacon of light
to the source of truth*

*The mind becomes weary
the body fragmented
when your heart's desire
is not followed*

*Follow the brightly lit
narrow passageway
of commitment to truth*

I want all of you

Surrender your will to divine will

Surrender

> *Why do you fight*
> *so painfully hard?*
>
> *Does the snake*
> *not shed?*
> *Does the butterfly*
> *not transform?*
>
> *So too, must you let*
> *the process unfold*
> *with the heartbeat*
> *of the divine*
>
> *Watch in amazement*
> *as the timing of life's*
> *synchronistic moments*
> *reveal their purpose.*
>
> *The choice is clear*
> *Surrender.*

We are not separate

Forever Yours

Let's walk together
on this journey of love
with certainty that
we are all connected

Your heart awakens
to the sound
of my voice
softly encouraging

The choice is yours
my blessed child
to journey as one
or part ways on the path

I will always be there
forever yours
waiting
for you to join me

Live in the present moment

Make Room for Me

Where do I fit
in your overcommitted life?

Are there any moments
I can wiggle into?

Pause, look around
and surprise I am there

Come to recognize how
effortlessly I appear

I make every moment
authentically joyous

And with time I
become a welcome guest

Thank you for giving me
a place of honour in your life

Let go of all

Follow Me

Sail with me to waters uncharted

> *Follow me, let me guide you,*
> *the voice within asks to be heard*

At times the sea may be rough
and at other times picture perfect

> *Follow me, let me guide you,*
> *the voice within asks to be heard*

The need to know what lies ahead
makes being patient ... intolerable

> *Follow me, let me guide you,*
> *the voice within asks to be heard*

Holding tightly to what you already know
in search of lasting comfort ... impossible

> *Follow me, let me guide you,*
> *the voice within asks to be heard*

Living lightly in the moment
with gentle awareness ... freedom

> *Follow me, let me guide you,*
> *the voice within is heard*

Breathe

Breath of Life

Remember the breath of life
as it nourishes your spirit

Remember to rejoice in song
as it uplifts your heart

Remember to express all emotion
as it releases your wisdom

Remember to speak your truth
as it reveals who you are

Breathe, often, openly, freely
joyously and lovingly

Breathe with ease
breathe, my child, breathe

An Invitation - Part III

Heart-Centred
Ways of Being

Heart-Centred
Ways of Being

Love

Loving

Divine interaction
Between you and me

Ego-free

Limitless

Forgiving heart

Love

I AM love.

To love means to understand with wisdom and grace how to be in relationship with yourself and others. Love is pure, open, giving, compassionate interaction with another human being. Only through me can you come to see this is possible.

I AM receptive love.

Come stand before me and know that I openly and unconditionally offer you the gift of my love. Like a child open and willing to engage with another from the heart, allow yourself to receive this precious gift.

Please accept this as the basis of our divine relationship. It is our loving relationship that will transform your relationships with others.

Through you I can assist others in knowing that they are worthy of receiving love that is beyond their understanding.

Love

I AM generous love.

This is the love you experience with a child that desires to connect from the heart giving love unconditionally and freely. Love such as this opens the hearts of those to which it is being given.

The open-hearted know they are worthy of receiving love immeasurable. With this wisdom you are endowed with the power to share this love openly with all living things.

I AM compassionate love.

Through you I can hold the hand of another; I can soothe with words of understanding; I can sing to awaken hearts; I can be present to listen with understanding and patience; I can reflect back the beauty I see in others.

In doing these things for you, I have shown you how to extend this to others. Thank you for allowing me to share the gift of compassionate love.

Love

I AM eternal love.

Through me you have eternal love – love that is limitless and everlasting. Know that you are loved beyond what you can comprehend in your human-ness.

It is in loving yourself that you come to love another. You have been offered this love so that you may share it with all living things. By extending this love anything and everything is possible. Open your heart to the possibility.

Heart-Centred
Ways of Being

Joy

Hallelujah

Your senses rejoice
emotions freely expressed

Hallelujah

Sing to the heavens
a song of surrender

The heart recognizes itself
in the familiar faces it sees
The animals, plants and birds
reach out welcoming you home

Let me show you the way
to the hallelujah
Open the gateway
and simply enter in

The path will be lit
voices encouraging
Leading you to the place
of joy within

Hallelujah!

Joy

Joy — Jubilation!

The stars sing and rejoice with the freedom of expression; a gift from the Heart of the Universe for simply being.

Meet me in the place where in your innocence you acknowledged and honoured all of who you are. Honour your path of the past as it has led you to the knowing of yourself today. Welcome all that you are to become.

I will guide the way so that you may clearly see your path and come to know true inner peace and joy. Embrace your journey. Enter knowing you are safe.

Open your heart and illuminate those places of shadow where the mind hesitates to wander; they are but fragments of journeys past asking to be reunited and made whole through the light you cast upon them.

Let energy bubble up through your heart to lighten the flow of feelings as they move through this open vessel of light; transforming and illuminating.

Joy

Let your heart sing and celebrate as you allow light to penetrate and illuminate your authentic self.

Emotions bathed in light emerge with honesty, clarity and insight. Grant yourself this gift of free expression of mind, body and spirit. Respectfully allow your experiences to move through you and release them like the ocean waves against the shore.

Begin to recognize the joy that accompanies the free expression of sorrow, frustration freed by laughter and the calm that lies beneath the storm. Discover the courage within yourself in moments of complacency.

Open to an innocent sincerity and engage in a heartfelt relationship with yourself and others. Let each living thing meet you where you are moment by moment.

It is in this place where your heart joins and honours all those you meet. As you present yourself with honesty and integrity others have the opportunity to meet you in this heart-centred space.

Joy

All creatures of the earth and sky open to greet you in this space of authenticity. Rejoice for the opportunity to let your heart unite with all living things as each sings a song of joy for the freedom to be.

It is here where you will find joy everlasting
you will find the *hallelujah!*

Heart-Centred
Ways of Being

Blessings

Illuminated

Light

Beyond universal systems
Beyond question or doubt
Contained in the "I"

See what I see

Brilliant radiance
Dances towards you
Floods your heart

Hear what I hear

Symphonic notes
Conducted joyfully with
Passionate resonance

Feel what I feel

Grateful intention
Increasingly committed
To benefit all

I AM illuminated

Blessings

Bless, bless, bless …

Bless all that you are.
Bless all that you have been.
Bless all that you are yet to become.

Bless, bless, bless …

Bless your loved ones.
Bless the trees, plants, rocks.
Bless the creatures great and small.
Bless the life-supporting waters of the earth.
Bless the sun, stars, the universe and worlds beyond.

Allow me to open your heart so that you see with eyes of gratitude. Give thanks for the rainbow of colours reflected back through you.

Treasure both your inner and outer vision as they will bring clarity to your life. The menagerie of images before you will assist and direct you towards the wisdom of your heart.

Blessings

Listen with ears of love and thankfulness. Listen as the sounds guide you to the natural rhythm here on earth and throughout the universe.

Notice the bird's song and how your instinctive rhythm attunes itself to the music you hear and feel. It is in this way that you attune to my heartbeat as it beats in unison with the Heart of the Universe.

Show your gratitude for the natural rhythm of the earth that expands and contracts with each breath it takes. Breathe deeply and align to the universal rhythmic flow of expansion and contraction.

Breathe in the life-sustaining air and give thanks for the support it offers you. With every breath, breathe me in and as you breathe out offer this gift of life to the plants that surround you.

Lay your hand gently upon the earth and bestow your blessing on all that you touch. It gives thanks for your loving caress.

Blessings

Honour all that presents itself before you and give it the loving attention that comes from a heart filled with thankfulness.

Everything you embrace is a part of you and all that exists. With an appreciative heart, utter sounds of gratitude and praise for all that you are. Let your words be poetic in nature so that they may reflect the mystery of the universe.

Share your words and the music of thanks with all. Sing joyfully to the glory of your spirit so that all may join you in this magnificent song of worship.

Thank you — for it is through these acts of appreciation that you come to understand who you are and who I AM within you.

Bless, bless, bless.

Heart-Centred
Ways of Being

Stillness

Touched

In the stillness appears
a radiant moment
The light dances
as if to say "take flight"

Move beyond this reality to the truth

Let yourself
be touched by the beauty
So subtle
yet so immense

Immerse yourself within

Caress each
moment gently
As the wind would
brush your cheek

Sing my child sing
to the glory of your spirit

Stillness

I AM softness, gentleness — quiet. Approach me with tenderness and humility. Sit with me awhile and I will meet you in this place of stillness.

In this place of quiet body and mind, you are able to connect with me in you. Together we can stand in a quiet receptive space where others may meet us.

Notice the quiet sturdy presence of a tree and its receptive nature; easily accessible and available for the birds and animals that come to rest on its branches. Only with its stationary presence can it share this gift of stillness and openness with others.

From this place of gentle awareness, I will reveal to you a deeper understanding of your connection with all things that is only possible in moments of quiet.

In time you may recognize the lack of separateness and the interplay of all on earth and throughout the universe. You may open your heart to the possibility that you and I are as one.

Stillness

Your breath is the same breath
of all that surrounds you.

Your voice in song is echoed back
by all in harmony with your song.

Your touch ripples energetically to be felt
across this earth and throughout the universe.

May you sense a feeling of support and coming home as you allow your senses to awaken to the experience of the world between the visible and the invisible.

In this place of stillness and absence of separateness you sense the natural rhythm of life. Watch with the same awareness as the animals that understand and flow with ease in this rhythmic universal dance.

In moments of stillness allow yourself to gracefully take part in this universal dance. Life becomes one of spontaneous joy for all who choose to engage in this light-hearted flow.

You come to recognize and deeply appreciate the beauty and abundance available to all. Your heart opens and extends blessings and gratitude for all that is.

Thank you for taking this moment to sit with me. I AM always here for you — waiting in the stillness.

Heart-Centred
Ways of Being

Humility

My Heart Calls

My heart calls out to you
sweet innocent babes

Know who you are
Know your influence
Know your power

Each of you will bring forth
my luminous presence

Know who you are
Know your influence
Know your power

Joyous, sustained, supported
graceful, vibrant movement

Know who you are
Know your influence
Know your power

Bestow your blessings, eagerly
generously, upon the gifts of life

Know who you are
Know your influence
Know your power

Humility

The strength that comes from knowing who you are is true humility. When you come to know me, you will understand how to be with your brothers and sisters.

I am the spark of divine love within you. I am a gift from the Heart of the Universe — the Creator of all; given so that my radiant light will live forever in you. Let your heart awaken and remember me. I am the light, the joy and the fullness of every expression in your life.

True strength is present through the knowing of your heart and your willingness to share a part of the light within your heart. Extend a loving hand, a kind word, a sincere smile to all you meet.

Rejoice through the song of your heart and let it soar to reach the hearts of all here on earth and throughout the universe. This song that you were given in the beginning is the voice of your heart. Use it to sing to the glory of your spirit and to the glory of all who are connected with you in that same spirit.

The heart will come to recognize itself and the light within, in its own time. Delight in knowing that what lives in you, lives in all. Address everyone you meet and everything you do with the same reverence and humility you extend to me, for I AM you. I AM all.

Through humility you possess an immovable and unstoppable strength rooted in truth.

There is no harsh word that can
contain the language of humility.

There is no intellectual retort that can
match the wisdom of the heart.

There is no destructive deed that can
remove the hand of loving-kindness.

Know that every thought, word and action that comes from a place of humility can rise above all. Offer the wisdom of the heart with the same patience and understanding that I have shown you.

Humility

Every act of humility is recognized and acknowledged. Through these generous acts the light within you meets the light within others.

This may not be apparent where you stand in this moment. Trust that with increased awareness, you will come to understand, that your actions reflect radiant light; actions that can transform any situation for the betterment of all.

Remain confident in this understanding of the power of humility. Watch the bird that builds its resilient nest from what appears to be fragile materials. So, it also is with humility and its deceptive outer appearance of gentle loving-kindness.

Present these humble acts from the heart and let them be the very thing that creates a pathway from heaven to earth. Listen carefully and you may hear – *thank you.*

Heart-Centred
Ways of Being

Compassion

Honour Yourself

Infinite
  Pure
    Commitment

Your heart is
the gateway
to love eternal

Courage
  Discipline
    Loyalty

Open your heart
to the power
that lies within

Kindness
  Tenderness
    Blessings

Let your heart
guide you with
grace and compassion

Peaceful
  Joyful
    Loving

Compassion

Like the stars that light up the night sky, know that my loving presence is always with you, even if temporarily hidden from your view. In time you will recognize this as the living light

the truth within you.

Let me love you with patience and understanding as you learn how to be in this world. See your human limitations as an opportunity to love yourself and to let others love you. Love yourself as I love you. Extend to yourself the same tenderness, understanding and patience.

Be gentle, kind and thoughtful toward yourself. Begin by opening your heart and allowing yourself to be treated with loving-kindness. With each kind and compassionate act, you extend towards yourself and others, your inner beauty blossoms and you move closer to understanding our relationship.

As you demonstrate compassion and gentleness toward yourself, others witness and recognize this within themselves.

Compassion

In honouring yourself you honour all those you meet. How then to honour yourself?

Create moments of quiet so you may hear my words of encouragement and loving-kindness.

Let go of any judgement or unnecessary criticism that keeps you from me. Let your heart guide you to know and love all that you are.

Release with ease that which no longer serves you. As the seasons change so do you. With every leaf that falls another grows anew. See these things drift by like the clouds in the sky.

Surround yourself with the people and things that remind you of my presence in you. Witness the reflection of your inner radiance in all you see.

Treat your human body with respect and dignity. Bless all that you consume and eliminate as part of your journey on earth. Extend gratitude to all that supports and sustains your life.

Compassion

Treat yourself as you would want others to treat you. Say to yourself the words that you would whisper to your lover.

Listen to the desire of your heart as if it were the greatest secret of the universe and meet this longing with enthusiasm and joy.

Treasure these gifts which are always available to you. You need only to seek them and they will be revealed.

Your spirit lightens and sings as it is recognized and honoured. It is here that you meet yourself and others in the place of heartfelt compassion. Cherish these moments for it is here that I join you.

Heart-Centred
Ways of Being

Wonderment

Imagination

Let me sense the world anew

With a fresh desire
to experience and relinquish
all previous notions
of understanding

 Wow!

 Neat!

 Awesome!

 Amazing!

Wonderment

Oh, the imagination, what a wonderful gift! Offered to you from the Heart of the Universe so that you may fulfill your purpose – your heart's desire; the very thing the Heart of the Universe desires for you. Use this gift wisely with the humility and respect for which it was given.

It can turn hills into mountains and valleys into canyons. To see things for the first time transforming all that is perceived.

Dust becomes earth
the breath – a gale
the babbling brook – a majestic waterfall
the ant – an ox and cart
the twig – a mighty oak tree
the feather – a powerful eagle.

Imagine as the light within appears as the universe.

Imagine letting go of all you understand this world to be. Let go of all images, ideas and impressions that were given to you. You have imagined what you see and experience before you. Trust me; you possess the ability to envision a new reality and perspective of yourself if you choose.

Wonderment

Together we can unite your heart and mind to bring this new existence into life. Join me in this adventure. Explore without limitation the world before you. Notice your presence and the response it commands from others and also how the presence of others commands a response from you.

Listen as I communicate to you through the language of the stars. Just as a newborn child has within itself the ability to learn any language, you also have the flexibility to understand and communicate through alternate means.

Begin to take your first step towards a different way of being in this world. Awaken your senses to your new surroundings. Oh, the wonder of new beginnings

new experiences

new possibilities.

Open yourself to the opportunities and passionately explore the world before you. Begin to recognize the interplay of all that exists and that you are an integral part of that existence.

Imagine that everything which appears to exist in solid form also exists in malleable form waiting for your imagination to transform it.

See yourself as not separate from all that exists. Know that this connectedness is influential in determining how you relate to yourself and everything on earth. With each step you take, notice the enormous power you have in shaping this world.

It is of great importance to operate from the heart
centred in *gratitude*
and *reverence* for all.

From this place you can begin to envision paradise – an idyllic world, united in vision from the place of truth.

Oh, the imagination, what a blessed gift!

Heart-Centred
Ways of Being

Grace

The Gift

Beautiful light
*   dance with me*

Show me the steps
*   of graceful movement*

Help me find delight
*   in the newness of each moment*

Grace

You are a blessed child of God
          a spark of divine light. I live in you and you in
me. It is through me that you come to recognize
                    your beauty
                    your magnificence
                    your heart.

By simply being in relationship with me you are alive; alive in spirit and free to *simply be*; at ease in each moment; receptive to the gift of grace; to simply be present in relationship with yourself, with others and all that surrounds you.

I have shown and continue to show you grace that surpasses all understanding. Be at peace with who you are, knowing you will always be worthy of kindness, forgiveness and love immeasurable through me.

As your heart comes to know and appreciate this gift, you may acknowledge it in others. With gratitude, extend to yourself and others the grace I have shown you.

Grace

Remember how precious and dear you are to all the lives you touch. I ask that you let your light within shine so that others may know their goodness.

The grace you offer has the ability to transform any perceived imperfection to perfection. Through you I am present and can touch the lives of all those you meet. Offer a loving hand, a kind word or a warm smile.

Willingly share this grace so that others may know that by simply being they are blessed. Let them witness the peace that comes from being in a grace-filled relationship.

Know that each moment blessed by grace is an opportunity to begin again. Grace forgives and sheds new light where before there was shadow. Let this light remind you of your worthiness to receive unconditional love and kindness.

Extend this light to all living creatures, the earth and the universe for they are also deserving of these gifts of grace.

Grace

The gift of grace has the power to transform all that cross its path. By purely offering this gift you allow yourself and others to transcend their human-ness and recognize the light within.

You are worthy of my love.
It is through me you can *simply be.*

Heart-Centred
Ways of Being

Playfulness

Lightly

Sing, dance, play

   Sing the song
   of your heart

Sing, dance, play

   Dance with others
   in the truth

Sing, dance, play

   Play joyfully within
   the universal rhythm

Sing, dance, play

   Giggle as I delight in
   showing you who I AM in you

Sing, dance, play – lightly

Playfulness

Light-hearted, joyful and playful; come and join me in this playground you call life.

Keep it simple and pure.
The heart knows no other way of being.

It is here that you find your existence to be light and joyous. Let me show you how to play as a child that finds life entertaining.

With a childlike heart that is fully engaged, your mind freely releases all concerns about earthly treasures. You are fully present in relationship to others and your surroundings. By simply being you allow these gifts of the physical to assist you, holding them lightly in a free exchange with others.

In this place your heart remains open and delighted. Smile, laugh and sing, for it is through these actions that your earthly presence becomes meaningful. Just as each song is unique, so is the distinctive expression of laughter and joy.

Playfulness

Listen to the birds of the air as they eagerly share their song at the break of dawn. Awaken each morning with a melody in your heart and lightness in your step. As your heart sings, your earthly body lightens.

It is through the heart that you come to recognize how to flow with ease in and out of situations and relationships.

Gracefully move through each day touching down softly on the earth.

Let all flow naturally, just as night turns to day and winter turns to spring.

Let each moment transition effortlessly into the next.

Release all that keeps you from being in this place of joy.

Breathe fully and heartily into all the spaces within, opening them to the free expression of laughter and song.

Laughing, smiling and being at ease with yourself and others becomes a natural way of interacting.

Your body responds to this feeling of spaciousness. Others are welcomed and enter willingly into this light-hearted space. It is here that you may join together in harmony; a symphonic masterpiece with each participant in their place, singing their unique heart song.

These simple gifts have been offered to gather the hearts of all in an opus of the grandest magnitude. Honour these priceless treasures as they awaken the truth within.

Truth is light and joyous and connects all harmoniously. Let this gift you have been given lead others to this knowing within themselves. All blessings flow as you walk in the truth.

Sing, dance and play along with me …

Epilogue

The Dance

The Dance

The earth sang its familiar tune that signaled it was time for change. Together in a wave of knowing the plants, animals and breezes responded.

This transformation was expected, just as one anticipates the breath of life; with each inhalation, there was trust that the exhalation would follow.

This natural rhythm communicated and felt by all life, ensured that existence would continue. Seasons came and went allowing a time for play and a time for rest.

With each inhalation the earth expanded with vitality; the colours, smells and sounds delighted the senses. With each exhalation came a sense of peace, calm and relaxation.

No thought was required, as each knew their part in the dance of the web called life. The movement was graceful and fluid and transitions were made with ease.

The Dance

There was a mutual understanding and one universal voice that resonated within. In the silence, all could clearly hear the song that heralded the changing of the seasons.

All co-existed in harmony, as each knew their place in the universal musical score. They listened with care and balanced each other, creating a symphonic masterpiece.

All was beautifully orchestrated and directed by a source that understood the value of each, as a necessary part of the whole. With the trust and respect of the players, they were able to unite and create with a common vision.

Each participant submitted and promised to sustain this vision as held by the Heart of the Universe; the vision that was to guide, direct and inform all. The vision held in the beginning, is now and always will be.

One voice, one vision, one heart – the Heart of the Universe – all glory and honour are yours now and forevermore.

CPSIA information can be obtained
at www.ICGtesting.com
Printed in the USA
LVHW090708071021
699798LV00001B/36